YOUR CONTRIBUTION TO SOCIETY

CORONA BREZINA

T0026781

Published in 2023 by The Rosen Publishing Group, Inc.
2544 Clinton St, Buffalo, NY 14224

First Edition

Editor: Greg Roza
Book Design: Michael Flynn
Interior Layout: Rachel Rising

Photo Credits: Cover, Blue Titan/Shutterstock.com; Cover, pp. 1, 3–6, 8, 10, 12–20, 22–24, 26, 28–32 tavizta/Shutterstock.com; p. 4 Gustavo Frazao/Shutterstock.com; p. 5 UfaBizPhoto/Shutterstock.com; p. 7 Rido/Shutterstock.com; p. 9 Michael Gordon/Shutterstock.com; p. 11 WENN Rights Ltd / Alamy Stock Photo; p. 12 Rawpixel.com/Shutterstock.com; p. 13 AnnGaysorn/Shutterstock.com; p. 14 Soloviova Liudmyla/Shutterstock.com; p. 15 VH-studio/Shutterstock.com; p. 16 Prostock-studio/Shutterstock.com; pp. 17, 22 Monkey Business Images/Shutterstock.com; p. 18 KieferPix/Shutterstock.com; p. 19 https://commons.wikimedia.org/wiki/File:2003_Special_Olympics_Opening_Crowd.JPG; p. 21 North Wind Picture Archives / Alamy Stock Photo; p. 23 William Perugini/Shutterstock.com; p. 25 LightField Studios/Shutterstock.com; p. 27 CarlosBarquero/Shutterstock.com; p. 28 Daniel M Ernst/Shutterstock.com; p. 29 Dmytro Zinkevych/Shutterstock.com.

Library of Congress Cataloging-in-Publication Data

Names: Brezina, Corona, author.
Title: Your contribution to society / Corona Brezina.
Description: Buffalo, New York : PowerKids Press, [2023] | Series: Spotlight on a fair and equal society | Includes index.
Identifiers: LCCN 2022038814 (print) | LCCN 2022038815 (ebook) | ISBN 9781538388389 (library binding) | ISBN 9781538388358 (paperback) | ISBN 9781538388396 (ebook)
Subjects: LCSH: Self-esteem--Juvenile literature. | Empathy--Juvenile literature. | Happiness--Juvenile literature.
Classification: LCC BF697.5.S46 B753 2023 (print) | LCC BF697.5.S46 (ebook) | DDC 158/.1--dc23/eng/20220824
LC record available at https://lccn.loc.gov/2022038814
LC ebook record available at https://lccn.loc.gov/2022038815

Manufactured in the United States of America

Some of the images in this book illustrate individuals who are models. The depictions do not imply actual situations or events.

CPSIA Compliance Information: Batch #CWPK23. For further information contact Rosen Publishing, New York, New York at 1-800-237-9932.

Find us on

CONTENTS

CHAPTER ONE

YOU MAKE A DIFFERENCE

Self-esteem is how you see yourself as a person. People with self-esteem are able to recognize their strengths. They believe in themselves and try harder. They can make a difference in the real world by using their talents to find a purpose.

Healthy self-esteem leads to **confidence**, positive thinking, and respect. A positive self-image gives people the power to work toward goals and deal with problems. It supports good **relationships** with others and allows you to be an **ally** to other people.

Do you feel good about yourself and recognize that you matter? If so, you have healthy self-esteem. This healthy self-esteem will help you believe in yourself and make positive contributions to your community.

Pride is a sense of satisfaction with things you do or who you are. You may be proud when you succeed at a project, help out at home, or **volunteer** with a food drive in your community. There are many ways you can make a difference and value your contributions to society.

CHAPTER TWO

SELF-AWARENESS

Self-awareness means understanding your emotions, thoughts, and values. This awareness influences how you see yourself as a person and as a part of social groups. Your own thoughts and feelings affect how you behave and engage with others.

Think about your **assets**, strengths, and resources. People who value you give you a sense of belonging and worth, seeing yourself through their eyes. You can give this feeling to others when you value them. Your awareness is the key to pride, confidence, and self-esteem.

Relationships build connections with people and teach you how to work and play respectfully. When you have healthy self-awareness, challenges help you grow and develop your strengths. Self-awareness can be a solution for problems. It can be the key to having a purpose, setting goals, and making a difference.

If you're confident in who you are, you'll feel comfortable sharing your ideas and thoughts with others.

CHAPTER THREE

IDENTIFYING NEGATIVE FEELINGS

Believing in yourself is a first step in making a difference for others. **Negative** feelings about who you are or what you can do are often the result of negative words, negative **attitudes**, and hurtful actions. If you hear often enough that you can't do something, you might believe it. If you are discouraged by others, you might give up and not even try.

The first step in changing negative thinking is recognizing it. Then, listen to those who see you through respectful eyes. Let the positive messages from allies like teachers, relatives, counselors, friends, or religious leaders be your focus. You have the potential to make a difference in big and small ways. You can work on recognizing your successes and knowing that you are doing your best. Grow with your challenges!

Negative feelings cause **stress** and worry. They can be managed when you check in on your feelings and tell yourself you're doing your best. The American basketball player and coach John Wooden said, "Work for progress, not perfection."

9

CHAPTER FOUR

POSITIVE THINKING

Perhaps a classroom in your school has a mural or sign on the wall that says: "Attitude is the key to success." This idea is supported by research about learning and everyday life. A positive outlook can help to accomplish positive results like happiness, success in school, good relationships, and sometimes even better health.

Positive thinking starts with you and a choice. You can choose to be in charge of your positive attitude and positive outcomes, even if you can't control events and problems. Positive thinking can take practice. Sometimes you might have to try to turn off your negative thoughts like you would turn off a TV. Changing your focus to your strengths and skills shifts your attitude to the positive, and you're taking charge of your response to situations. You are ready to say, "I can do this!"

Amanda Southworth was 13 when she created AnxietyHelper, a mental health guidebook for teens. Southworth reached out to others who also had self-esteem issues.

CHAPTER FIVE

LOOKING IN THE MIRROR

Kids between the ages of 9 and 12 may spend an average of six hours a day using social media. You might take selfies, post on TikTok, watch for likes, or share video. You might experience judgments, comparisons, and messages about your appearance. Some people experience stress, **anxiety**, and negative feelings related to how they look, expecially related to social media. Better self-esteem can be the answer to this problem.

Confidence, self-respect, and positive thinking might be difficult to manage if social pressure targets you or your friends. Bystanders might witness mean, hurtful speech or actions involving how someone looks. However, you can do the right thing and help by making the decision to be an ally and step up.

Healthy bodies come in many different shapes and sizes. We all should celebrate this and accept who we are.

CHAPTER SIX

TAKE CARE OF YOURSELF

It's important for people to eat a healthy diet, exercise, and get enough sleep. These habits will help you stay physically healthy.

However, your mental and emotional health are important too. It's normal to feel stressed sometimes. Stress is what you feel when you're worried or nervous. If you're feeling stressed, ask a parent or teacher for help. There are ways to deal with stress. Take time to relax and spend time doing hobbies you enjoy. Learn to manage your time so that you can balance your different activities.

Taking care of yourself can mean spending time on enjoyable activities that help you manage stress in your life, whether it's by relaxing or getting creative.

Strong relationships with your family and friends can help keep you healthy and happy. If you're feeling blue, make an extra effort to spend time with people you care about.

CHAPTER SEVEN

DO YOUR BEST

Healthy self-esteem and a sense of pride can help you reach your own personal best. This means using your strengths and skills to **achieve** things that mean something to you. For some people, going for their personal best involves having a sense of purpose and helping make the world a better place.

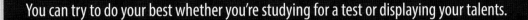
You can try to do your best whether you're studying for a test or displaying your talents.

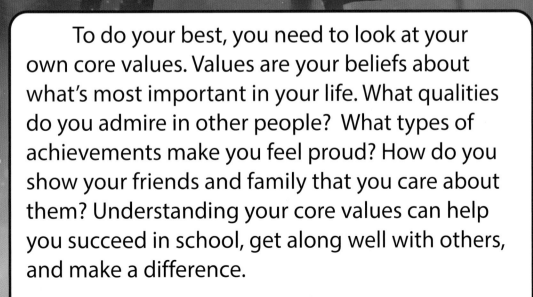

To do your best, you need to look at your own core values. Values are your beliefs about what's most important in your life. What qualities do you admire in other people? What types of achievements make you feel proud? How do you show your friends and family that you care about them? Understanding your core values can help you succeed in school, get along well with others, and make a difference.

CHAPTER EIGHT

BUILD YOUR CONFIDENCE

Self-confidence is part of having healthy self-esteem. Self-confidence is a belief that you can achieve a certain goal or overcome difficulties. If you have solid self-confidence, you'll feel more prepared to take on challenges, solve problems, and be an ally to others.

Self-confidence also affects your relationships with others. You're more likely to reach out to other people if you feel that you'll enjoy spending time with them. You'll form closer friendships if you believe that you can count on your friends through good times and bad.

The Special Olympics, founded by Eunice Kennedy Shriver, provide athletes with intellectual or physical differences with a chance to show off their athletic **abilities**. The first games were held in Chicago in 1968.

Your self-confidence will grow stronger with experience. If you succeed in achieving your goals, you'll be likelier to expect future successes. If you don't succeed in a goal, don't view it as failure. Look at it as a chance to learn. Try again, using what you've learned from your experience.

CHAPTER NINE

SET SOME GOALS

Setting goals and reaching for them can boost self-esteem and help provide a sense of pride in your achievements. Working toward goals gives you a sense of purpose.

Start out by setting small goals. Do you dream about helping homeless people? You could start by volunteering at a local soup kitchen. You might be able to join or **donate** money or supplies to a local organization that fights homelessness.

People often set very high goals but have no plan for achieving them, thereby setting themselves up for failure. If you have big dreams for the future, look at these as long-term goals. Break them down into smaller short-term goals that you can start working on right away. You'll feel a sense of achievement as you make day-to-day progress toward your long-term goal.

Writer Louisa May Alcott once said this about her motivation for setting goals: "Far away there in the sunshine are my highest **aspirations**. I may not reach them, but I can look up and see their beauty, believe in them, and try to follow where they lead."

CHAPTER TEN

REACH OUT

Are you ready to make a contribution to a fair and equal society? Growing up can mean beginning to think more about what others need and how you can share your time and abilities with others, including your family, friends, and community. Self-worth, confidence, and talents are assets that you can't see but can put to good use to help others.

People with good self-esteem are comfortable sharing their thoughts and feelings and will reach out to friends when they need support.

Look around your home, your school, your neighborhood, and your community. Can you make a connection or take an opportunity to help solve a problem or make a positive change? Are there groups of people you know that are already engaged in making a difference and may need you as an ally? Reaching out to trusted teachers or family might open your possibilities for community service. Offer to help. You can be a proud part of action for a better world.

CHAPTER ELEVEN

CONNECT WITH OTHERS

Having good self-esteem can help you keep strong relationships with others. People with healthy self-esteem are able to form positive relationships that are supportive and accepting.

If you're able to recognize your own strengths and weaknesses, you're more likely to accept the **traits** that make each of your friends special. If you aren't too hard on yourself for your own faults, you're more likely to be positive and supportive of the other people around you.

Healthy self-esteem can help you build your relationship skills. Here are a few examples of people skills that can be improved with practice:

- Working with others
- Setting boundaries
- Communicating clearly
- Using active listening
- Resolving conflicts
- Showing gratitude

Forming good relationships when you're young can help establish a lifelong pattern of healthy relationships with family and friends.

Spend time with friends who accept and respect you. Positive and supportive relationships help keep people happy and healthy.

CHAPTER TWELVE

CELEBRATE DIFFERENCES

When you know people who are different from you, you can better understand their experiences and feelings. You can accept and respect a diversity of viewpoints and traditions. Diversity refers to differences among people based on factors such as race, gender, age, or religion. You could feel pride in your family, your culture, or your own special talents or strengths. You may try harder to succeed if you know that your achievements will serve as a source of pride for people who share your **identity** and values.

Embracing diversity isn't always easy. In school, you may tend to hang out with friends with similar backgrounds and interests. Try to get to know your peers who are different from you. Wherever you are, treat everyone with respect whether they're similar or different from you.

You'll be more likely to open up to other people if you're not worried that they will judge you or reject you.

CHAPTER THIRTEEN

GIVE BACK

If you have healthy self-esteem and a sense of pride, you may wonder how you can make a difference in the world around you. Small actions can be very meaningful. Are you good at math? You could join or even start an afterschool homework club to help others who might be struggling in math.

Volunteering gives you a chance to be of service and try out new experiences. You'll be able to connect with other people who care about a shared cause, whether that's cleaning up litter or working on a food drive. Helping others can give you a sense of purpose. Ask your parents or teacher for volunteering ideas. Or find a way to make a difference near you online at **kidsthatdogood.com**.

CHAPTER FOURTEEN

MOVE FORWARD

Recognizing that you make a difference is important in believing in yourself and leading a purposeful life. Keeping a caring and positive attitude opens your eyes to possibilities. You can contribute to your community and your world.

Self-confidence can help you achieve successes that boost your pride and sense of your personal power to make positive change. You can prove your own worth to yourself with every goal you set and achieve. If you're comfortable with who you are, you're more likely to accept and respect diversity in the people around you.

As a young adult, learning now to think positively and act confidently can help you throughout your life. You'll be able to take advantage of opportunities, handle setbacks in life, and build honest, supportive relationships with others.

GLOSSARY

ability (uh-BIH-luh-tee) Being able to do something.

achieve (uh-CHEEV) To succeed at something through hard work.

ally (AA-ly) Someone who stands up for someone else.

anxiety (ang-ZIH-uh-tee) Fear or nervousness about what might happen.

aspiration (aa-spuh-RAY-shun) A strong desire to achieve something great.

asset (AA-seht) A resource, or something that can be used.

attitude (AA-tuh-tood) A feeling or way of thinking that affects a person's behavior.

confidence (KAAN-fuh-dens) Belief in one's own abilities, strengths, or ideas.

donate (DOH-nayt) To give something in order to help a person or organization.

identity (ai-DEN-uh-tee) A person's sense of how they think of themselves.

negative (NEH-guh-tiv) Harmful, bad, or unwanted.

relationship (ree-LAY-shuhn-ship) The way in which two or more people are connected.

stress (STRES) Something that causes strong feelings of worry.

trait (TRAYT) A quality that makes one person or thing different from another.

volunteer (vohl-uhn-TEER) To do something to help because you want to do it.

INDEX

PRIMARY SOURCE LIST

Page 9
Statue of UCLA coach John Wooden. Photograph. May 7, 2017. UCLA campus, Los Angeles, California. Held by Shutterstock.

Page 19
Special Olympics World Games opening ceremonies. Photograph. 2003. Croke Park, Dublin, Ireland. Held by Wikimedia Commons.

Page 21
Louisa May Alcott. Hand-colored woodcut. 19th century. North Wind Picture Archives.

TITLES IN THIS SERIES

ACCEPTANCE, RESPECT, AND APPRECIATION OF DIFFERENCE

ALLIES WORK TOGETHER

CONNECTING WITH OTHERS

EMPATHY FOR ALL

EQUITY AND FAIRNESS

JUSTICE FOR ALL

OUR UNIQUE IDENTITIES

RESPECTING OUR DIFFERENCES

SOCIAL JUSTICE THROUGH ACTIVISM

STANDING UP FOR HUMAN RIGHTS

VALUING THE CONTRIBUTIONS OF OTHERS

YOUR CONTRIBUTION TO SOCIETY

PowerKiDS
press

ISBN: 9781538388358

9 781538 388358